WHAT'S IN THE
BIBLE
(FOR ME)?

50 readings and reflections

Lucy Moore

The Bible Reading Fellowship
15 The Chambers, Vineyard
Abingdon OX14 3FE
brf.org.uk

The Bible Reading Fellowship (BRF) is a Registered Charity (233280)

ISBN 978 0 85746 760 7
First published 2020
10 9 8 7 6 5 4 3 2 1 0

Text by Lucy Moore 2020
This edition © The Bible Reading Fellowship 2020
Cover and inside illustrations by Rebecca J Hall

The author asserts the moral right to be identified as the author of this work

Acknowledgements
Scripture quotations are taken from the Contemporary English Version. New Testament
© American Bible Society 1991, 1992, 1995. Old Testament © American Bible Society
1995. Anglicisations © British & Foreign Bible Society 1996. Used by permission.

Every effort has been made to trace and contact copyright owners for material used
in this resource. We apologise for any inadvertent omissions or errors, and would ask
those concerned to contact us so that full acknowledgement can be made in the future.

A catalogue record for this book is available from the British Library

Printed and bound in the UK by Zenith Media NP4 0DQ

Contents

Introduction 5
How to use this book 7

OLD TESTAMENT

1 Home 10
2 Leaving home 12
3 Go! 14
4 Exit visa refused 16
5 Desert trek 18
6 They think it's all over… 20
7 Colourful characters 22
8 Songs for the journey 24
9 Cliff edge 26
10 Dreaming of home 28
11 Breakdown 30
12 Refugee status 32
13 Return journey 34
14 Radio silence 36

NEW TESTAMENT

15 The longest journey 40
16 A time of journeys 42
17 Baptism 44
18 Journey into the desert 46
19 Follow me 48

20 Journey away from home 50
21 Teaching on the way 52
22 Healing on the way 54
23 Back to the wilderness 56
24 A different sort of wilderness walk 58
25 Changed lives on the way 60
26 Off you go! 62
27 Hospitality on the way 64
28 Staying put 66
29 Stories from the road 68
30 Stories for the road home 70
31 So near! 72
32 And yet so far! 74
33 Not a picnic in the park 76
34 Journey to Jerusalem 78
35 Food for the journey ahead 80
36 Journey to the cross 82
37 Journey from death to life 84
38 Journey of discovery 86
39 Get going! 88
40 Rocket launcher 90
41 Making it up as we go along 92
42 The going gets tough 94
43 An unexpected passenger 96
44 A bigger map 98
45 Changing the map 100
46 Working it out as we go along 102
47 Steering a course 104
48 Navigating wrong turns 106
49 The way, the destination 108
50 Eyes on the horizon 110

Introduction

Life. It's complicated. If you tried to describe the journey you've been on so far in your own life, what would you include? What would you miss out? How would you select what was important? It could never be a complete picture and would inevitably be subjective. And that's just one life journey! What if you were trying to describe the life journey of a whole nation lasting thousands of years? Or, even more complicated, the life journey of the human race? Impossible!

So it's not surprising that the Bible is a complicated book – or rather, set of books. It might feel at first sight as if you're looking at an explorer's workroom, covered with maps, letters, stories, legends, copies of songs, odd scribblings that don't make sense. Where do you even start reading?

What's in the Bible (for me)? is only one particular 'take' on what the Bible is about – it's just one viewpoint. It picks up the idea of a 'journey' to follow through. There are plenty of other ideas we could follow through instead, but to skim through 66 books that cover some 4,000 years in just 50 short chunks, one idea is enough!

We'll follow this idea of journeys loosely through the 50 selected passages to help us understand a tiny fraction of this beautiful, frustrating, inspiring, challenging, compelling, illuminating, life-giving, puzzling book of books, reading a little at a time and letting it sink in.

The journey of a family leaving home...

the journey of the family God chose to light the way for others to follow...

the journey of an entire nation nearer to and further from God...

the journey of God from heaven to earth and back...

the journey of a new way of living spreading across the Mediterranean world...

the journey of a human being like you or me towards a destination that becomes clearer with each step...

What's in the Bible (for me)? explores the big journey of the Bible. And maybe, as we see the bigger picture, it will help us understand our own journey.

How to use this book

Each page gives a short Bible passage to read followed by an explanation or reflection about what's going on in it, and a question or challenge to take into the day ahead. There's also a **#jesusjourney** question to use as a discussion starter if you're going through the book as a group or to throw out on social media to see if the wider community has more wisdom to offer.

On each page, you'll find the passage, the book it comes from with the chapter number, and a comment on why I think it's important or an explanation of what's going on in it. The printed verses are in the Contemporary English Version (CEV) translation, but you might like to have a look at some other translations and find the one that works the best for you and your family. The Bible Gateway website (**biblegateway.com**) has lots of different translations and is very easy to find your way around.

We've had to shorten some passages because of space restrictions. The three dots (…) show where words have been left out, but you can always go and look up the passages in a Bible or online to see them in full.

You might want to read one of these pages every day for a month or so, to give yourself time to think about each one properly.

Or you might read it all in one sitting to get the broad sweep. You might read it on your own, or together as a family and talk about it. You might want to start with the New Testament (page 40) and go back to the Old Testament afterwards. The booklet will fit in your bag or pocket, so it can go with you to the place where you have time to read it – on the bus or train, in the cafe or playground or on your lunch break. Scribble on it; wave it at your local minister or Christian friend and make them answer your questions or listen to your theories. Safe travels!

Old Testament

1

Home

The Lord made a garden in a place called Eden, which was in the east, and he put the man there.

The Lord God placed all kinds of beautiful trees and fruit trees in the garden. Two other trees were in the middle of the garden. One of the trees gave life – the other gave the power to know the difference between right and wrong…

The Lord God put the man in the Garden of Eden to take care of it and to look after it. But the Lord told him, 'You may eat fruit from any tree in the garden, except the one that has the power to let you know the difference between right and wrong. If you eat any fruit from that tree, you will die before the day is over!'

GENESIS 2

If you live at a time when your culture is deeply connected to the planet, its plants, animals, seasons and rhythms, and you want to describe how the world began, you're not going to start with the Big Bang. Story is much older than science as we understand it today. It holds a different but equally valid sort of truth. Look at what the opening chapters of the first book of the Bible tell us about who God is, in what spirit the heavens and earth were created, what God's relationship with human beings was in the beginning and how God meant the planet to be.

One aspect of this perfect state of being is that we see God and humans working together in a beautiful garden, enjoying each other's company and the place made with them in mind. Work is a pleasure. Other people are a delight. God is present and active. There are safe boundaries. The rhythm of work and rest is perfectly balanced. The natural world thrives. It is an entirely content, purposeful and fulfilling state of being. It is home.

Think about your own home today and thank God for anything in it that reflects Eden.

#jesusjourney
Eden: the best thing about it was…

2

Leaving home

The woman stared at the fruit. It looked beautiful and tasty. She wanted the wisdom that it would give her, and she ate some of the fruit. Her husband was there with her, so she gave some to him, and he ate it too...

The Lord said, 'These people now know the difference between right and wrong, just as we do. But they must not be allowed to eat fruit from the tree that lets them live forever.' So the Lord God sent them out of the Garden of Eden, where they would have to work the ground from which the man had been made. Then God put winged creatures at the entrance to the garden and a flaming, flashing sword to guard the way to the life-giving tree.

GENESIS 3

It takes just three chapters for the perfect home and its perfect relationships to fall apart. The people ignored the one restriction God gave them and ate the fruit they had been told to leave alone. The story tries to explain what it means to be a human being through carefully crafted storytelling, where deep and unpalatable truths lie beneath talking snakes and forbidden fruit.

The writer of Genesis is brutally honest about humanity. He tells us it was the choice of human beings to kick against the boundaries rather than trust God, and that decision has tough consequences. Eden is still there but is now impossible to re-enter. Humans now need to experience pain. What used to come naturally is now gruelling and agonising. The perfect balance has ended. 'Being' has changed to 'going'. The journey has begun.

If you've ever watched someone you love leaving you – a child going to school for the first time, a friend emigrating – you know something of how God felt when those wonderful companions and creations disappeared through the gate of Eden. This story, known as 'the fall', is the start of the end. But even here, we can spot clues of God's plan to bring God's people home again eventually. God will rescue us. It's who God is.

Which of your choices do you most regret? How much do you believe God can rescue you from its consequences?

#jesusjourney
    Eating the fruit: good choice, bad choice?

3

Go!

The Lord said to Abram: 'Leave your country, your family, and your relatives and go to the land that I will show you. I will bless you and make your descendants into a great nation. You will become famous and be a blessing to others. I will bless anyone who blesses you, but I will put a curse on anyone who puts a curse on you. Everyone on earth will be blessed because of you.'

Abram was seventy-five years old when the Lord told him to leave the city of Haran. He obeyed and left with his wife Sarai, his nephew Lot, and all the possessions and slaves they had gotten while in Haran... They came to the land of Canaan.

GENESIS 12

If human beings messed up God's perfect plan for them, perhaps God's rescue can happen through human beings. The foundations need to be laid many years in advance, if we are to stand a chance of understanding what the rescuer is doing. (The book of Genesis was probably written down about 1,400 years before Jesus was born but describes events that happened long before the time of writing.)

Here, we see one of the first steps towards the big rescue plan: God calls one person, Abram, a.k.a. Abraham, to leave his home and set out on a journey. Where? 'To the land that I will show you' – in other words, Abram needs to trust God enough to set out without being told all the details. This isn't just a journey through geography; more significantly, it's a journey towards a friendship with God. And for this to happen, there is a call from God, a promise and a choice of whether to stay with the safe and familiar or whether to leave with nothing but God's promise.

Why? 'Everyone on earth will be blessed because of you': Abram and his family will be the funnel through which God pours life in all its fullness – on everyone.

In the Bible, we often see an important journey starting through one person trusting in God; another example might be Mary, Jesus' mother.

Look out for ways to bless people today.

#jesusjourney
   Step out in faith or wait for proof?

4

Exit visa refused

One day, Moses [journeyed] to Sinai, the holy mountain.
There an angel of the Lord appeared to him from a
burning bush. Moses saw that the bush was on fire,
but it was not burning up... When the Lord saw Moses
coming near the bush, he called him by name, and Moses
answered, 'Here I am'...

The Lord said: 'I have seen how my people are suffering
as slaves in Egypt... I feel sorry for them, and I have come
down to rescue them from the Egyptians. I will bring my
people out of Egypt into a country where there is good
land.'

EXODUS 3

The story of God's relationship with Abraham's family has
moved on, marked by plenty of adventures and by God making
a solemn promise of faithfulness (technical term: 'covenant')
to Abraham along the way. Abraham's descendants did settle
in the land God prepared for them, but ended up (long story)
as slave labourers to the Egyptians – in a place far from home,
working for brutal taskmasters and vulnerable to exploitation
to the point of their children being slaughtered. This was hardly

God's intention for the family which was meant to be happy and whole, and who would make the whole earth happy and whole.

In Exodus 3, we see one of Abraham's descendants, Moses, being asked to trust God's call and rescue God's family in his turn. God again chooses to rescue God's people through one person's faith. The dramatic journey Moses took the people on – out of Egypt, through the Red Sea and into freedom – is a story told and retold by Jewish people every Passover and reinterpreted by Christians in every service of Holy Communion and in baptism.

This journey of Moses and the people is one from slavery to freedom through water. Look out for water elsewhere on this epic journey.

Where do you see modern-day slavery around you? Who is working to 'set my people free' today?

#jesusjourney
   Do we ever knowingly choose slavery over freedom?

5

Desert trek

There in the desert [the Israelites] started complaining to Moses and Aaron, 'We wish the Lord had killed us in Egypt. When we lived there, we could at least sit down and eat all the bread and meat we wanted. But you have brought us out here into this desert, where we are going to starve.'

The Lord said to Moses, 'I will send bread down from heaven like rain. Each day the people can go out and gather only enough for that day.'

EXODUS 16

Moses and the people are safe from the Egyptians, but they now need to journey to the promised land. And after all the excitement of escaping from Egypt, it's very, very boring. It's a desert. Unless you're David Attenborough, it's very, very dull. It needs crossing. And God leads them round and round the desert, not in a nice, tidy, speedy straight line. God provides a pillar of cloud and a pillar of fire for them to follow, so they can be sure of God's guidance. It's God who provides manna and quail to eat day by day and water in the wilderness. It's God who gives Moses the ten commandments to help the people work out what it means to journey together as people who belong to

God and to each other. It's God who keeps them on their desert journey for 40 years.

Is a journey always about getting from A to B in the shortest possible time? Is this wilderness experience perhaps taking the people on a different sort of journey? If you relied on God for direction, food and drink every single day for 40 years, what might that do to your relationship with that God? When Jesus taught his followers to pray, 'Give us today our daily bread', do you think he had this story in mind?

#jesusjourney
    Daily bread, daily slog. How much excitement do we expect?

6

They think it's all over...

One day, Joshua was near Jericho when he saw a man standing some distance in front of him. The man was holding a sword, so Joshua walked up to him and asked, "Are you on our side or on our enemies' side?"

'Neither,' he answered. 'I am here because I am the commander of the Lord's army.'

Joshua fell to his knees and bowed down to the ground. 'I am your servant,' he said. 'Tell me what to do.'

'Take off your sandals,' the commander answered. 'This is a holy place.' So Joshua took off his sandals.
JOSHUA 5

The journey was over, surely? The desert was behind them. All that lay between God's people and the promised land was the River Jordan. Joshua has taken over as leader of the Israelites and carefully, prayerfully, led the people through the river to the homeland God promised them. (Another step-change through water!) But arriving doesn't mean everything is over. In fact, it's yet another ending that is a new beginning.

To modern eyes, the story of conquering the land and destroying the previous inhabitants makes for uncomfortable reading. Genocide appears to take place (although as the story unfolds, it's clear that the apparent slaughter is much less wholesale than is suggested here). This is a very specific situation and not meant as a justification for wiping out anyone who stands in our way. It could, however, be a picture of the unstoppable growth of God's kingdom. Joshua's encounter here with the commander of the Lord's army, who refuses to take sides, shows us there is something going on in a different dimension from that of geography.

What a line of rescuer-leaders is building up already! Abraham, Moses and now Joshua, all pioneers in their different ways. Joshua shares a name with a much later and even greater rescuer-leader who will do all that his great-great-great (...) grandparents did, but without making a single wrong turn. ('Joshua' and 'Jesus' are the same name.)

Whenever we think we've 'arrived', we realise there is now a different sort of journey to go on. How content are you, as you follow Jesus, to be always on the move?

#jesusjourney
When is an ending a beginning?

7

Colourful characters

Deborah... was a prophet and a leader of Israel during those days. She would sit under Deborah's Palm Tree... where Israelites would come and ask her to settle their legal cases.

Deborah sent word for [Barak]... When he arrived, she said: 'I have a message for you from the Lord God of Israel! You are to get together an army of ten thousand men from the Naphtali and Zebulun tribes and lead them to Mount Tabor. The Lord will trick Sisera into coming out to fight you at the Kishon River. Sisera will be leading King Jabin's army as usual, and they will have their chariots, but the Lord has promised to help you defeat them.'

JUDGES 4

Settling into the promised land brought conflicts and tensions with the surrounding nations. God's people found themselves at war with their enemies and at risk of compromising their unique covenant status with God. Through the history books of the Bible, including Judges, Samuel, Kings and Chronicles, we see God staying faithful to the chosen people of God and giving them every chance to make the inner journey back towards their God, while the people make disastrous choices over and over again.

The books are filled with the colourful characters sent by God to lead his people, including Deborah here. They're cracking stories, if also deeply depressing, as God's people and leaders fail to live lives that honour God. Who will be the great judge and king to rescue God's people and lead them into a life of blessing that blesses others? Each leader messes up. Even the golden boy, King David himself, makes catastrophic mistakes. But the stage is set for a judge, king and rescuer (technical term 'the Messiah'), who will come from the same family as David but who will come and get it right. The failings of all the others who went before him make his success all the more vivid.

Who is a colourful character influencing your life, who leads people into lifestyles that bless them and bless others? Is there something you can do today to affirm them or thank them for their leadership?

#jesusjourney
Good leaders: safe or wild?

8
Songs for the journey

From out of a storm, the Lord said to Job: 'Why do you talk so much when you know so little? Now get ready to face me! Can you answer the questions I ask? How did I lay the foundation for the earth? Were you there? Doubtless you know who decided its length and width. What supports the foundation? Who placed the cornerstone, while morning stars sang, and angels rejoiced?'

JOB 38

The Bible is made up of all sorts of books. Some map out the physical journey that God's people travelled. Some map out the rules they tried to live by. Some describe characters to inspire us, reassure us or warn us. And some of the books map out what's going on in the human heart, giving language to the unnameable movements in our soul, in our spirit. If the Bible were simply a book of rules or of history, it might feel very bleak. But in books like Job, we find story and poetry helping us through a different sort of terrain.

Job sets the mystery of human suffering into a framework of story and poetry, not in order to provide an answer to the unanswerable, but to give expression to that mystery, within the story of God and God's people. Human beings have long understood that words can be an important part of the healing process, and here we see ancient words of great beauty reaching into the imagination to acknowledge something of the agony and joy of any person's journey through life.

Which writer, artist or musician best expresses the longings of your heart at the moment? Try to find time to enjoy their work today.

#jesusjourney
   Which artist's creativity lets your soul travel on?

9

Cliff edge

The Lord said: 'I will sing a song about my friend's vineyard that was on the side of a fertile hill... He hoped [the grapes] would be sweet, but bitter grapes were all it produced... Now I will let you know what I am going to do... It will turn into a desert, neither pruned nor hoed; it will be covered with thorns and briars. I will command the clouds not to send rain. I am the Lord All-Powerful! Israel is the vineyard, and Judah is the garden I tended with care. I had hoped for honesty and for justice, but dishonesty and cries for mercy were all I found.'
ISAIAH 5

If you saw someone about to walk off a cliff by mistake, you'd probably do all you could to call them back from the edge. The prophets had the uncomfortable job of telling people who, by and large, did not want to be told that they were walking towards a cliff edge. The books of the prophets are full of warnings to get back on to the right road – to live for justice and righteousness, not bloodshed and exploitation.

The writings are shot through with glimpses of that future rescuer who won't sell God short, but will lead people into the life they are meant to live. God has a plan to rescue you, the prophets say. But avoid the disaster in the first place! Choose God's way, not that path… no… really, really not that path…! However, even with visions of imminent catastrophe graphically described, even with the prophets using every means at their disposal, including underpants (I kid you not – check out Jeremiah 13), people don't listen and carry on towards the cliff edge.

How uncomfortable do you find it to speak the truth – or to hear the truth – about situations of injustice today?

#jesusjourney
 What cliff edge can you see someone – maybe you – walking perilously close to?

10

Dreaming of home

> The Lord will teach us his Law from Jerusalem, and we will obey him. He will settle arguments between distant and powerful nations. They will pound their swords and their spears into rakes and shovels; they will never again make war or attack one another. Everyone will find rest beneath their own fig trees or grape vines, and they will live in peace. This is a solemn promise of the Lord All-Powerful. Others may follow their gods, but we will always follow the Lord our God.
>
> MICAH 4

This passage describes something of God's longing for humanity. It expresses God's understanding of that deep human need to have a home. The part about the vine and fig tree meant a great deal for me when I was living in a place that didn't feel like home. Micah told me it was okay to want more than a roof and four walls. It wasn't unreasonable to long for a home. God wants peace for all people on earth. God longs for them to be at home, to be safe, to settle, to be surrounded by plenty to eat and drink and to have the freedom to follow their God or gods as they choose.

The tiny nation of Israel did not see their role as one of blending in with the nations around them. They saw themselves as set apart to worship God, to live distinctively, to demonstrate, in the rules they lived by, who their God was. They had their covenant relationship with God, the ten commandments (Exodus 20) and whole books of other rules to live by, designed to help them to live lives pleasing to God. In this time of settled living, no longer on a journey, the dangers of forgetting God were even greater than when they were relying on God day by day during their epic journey through the desert.

Which parts of your life feel settled? Give thanks to God for the blessings of safety, peace and plenty: the blessings of home that foreshadow our forever home that we'll reach one day.

#jesusjourney
   What rule in life is written on your heart?

11

Breakdown

I, the Lord, say... 'You refused to listen to me, and now I will let you be attacked by nations from the north, and especially by my servant, King Nebuchadnezzar of Babylonia. You and other nearby nations will be destroyed and left in ruins forever. Everyone who sees what has happened will be shocked, but they will still make fun of you.'

JEREMIAH 25

The time for warnings was over. Everything God had warned of came to happen. Enemy armies marched on the land and defeated God's people, who were taken away into exile to faraway Babylon. The heart of the land was ripped out as the temple was plundered and all but a handful of people taken captive. To a people whose identity and security in God was tied up with their physical land, especially the city of Jerusalem, this was cataclysmic devastation. It must have seemed as if their journey as a nation was over.

God's people were meant to be living in 'covenant' together with their God: within the bounds of a firm promise on either side. They had broken their promise of faithfulness and it must have seemed as though God had finally lost patience and broken God's side of the promise too. But God's faithfulness to humanity never fails, and even in the middle of prophecies of disaster, Jeremiah glimpses the new covenant God is preparing, understood from the inside out: 'Here is the new agreement that I, the Lord, will make with the people of Israel: I will write my laws on their hearts and minds' (Jeremiah 31:33).

Think about faithfulness today.

#jesusjourney

Is your heart more like an album cover or a graffiti wall?

12

Refugee status

Beside the rivers of Babylon we thought about Jerusalem, and we sat down and cried. We hung our small harps on the willow trees. Our enemies had brought us here as their prisoners, and now they wanted us to sing and entertain them. They insulted us and shouted, 'Sing about Zion!' Here in a foreign land, how can we sing about the Lord? Jerusalem, if I forget you, let my right hand go limp. Let my tongue stick to the roof of my mouth, if I don't think about you above all else.

PSALM 137

Humiliated, lost, uprooted, off-course, dispossessed, without a hope of getting back on track, the people of God are out in the desert once again, centuries after their ancestors wandered the desert with Moses. Babylon is where they live, but it is not home. It's a land of foreign gods, weird food, unfamiliar practices and all-powerful rulers. They need to learn from rock bottom what it means to be faithful to God when all their dignity, routines, aids, structures and buildings have been stripped away.

Following Jesus takes us on a journey that never ends. Every stopping place is temporary, though it may seem at the time to last a lifetime. The devastating exile in Babylon could have been seen as the final punishment for unfaithfulness, or as the chance to start again and learn afresh what faithfulness meant to the new generation. When a community went so terribly wrong, could there be a way to find their way home? When we go wrong, is the inevitable consequence of that wrong choice the final word?

If you were dumped on a desert island with nothing and no one, how do you imagine your journey with Jesus would turn out?

#jesusjourney
   How can you sing the Lord's song in a strange land?

13

Return journey

The Lord kept his promise by having Cyrus [King of Persia] send this official message to all parts of his kingdom... 'The Lord God of heaven, who is also the God of Israel, has made me the ruler of all nations on earth. And he has chosen me to build a temple for him in Jerusalem, which is in Judah. The Lord God will watch over and encourage any of his people who want to go back to Jerusalem and help build the temple...' Many people felt that the Lord God wanted them to help rebuild his temple, and they made plans to go to Jerusalem.

EZRA 1

The time of exile did indeed come to an end. It took 70 years! But at last, some of the people of God could go 'home'. The very concept of home had changed over the 70 years. There was so much to rediscover and to work out what to hang on to and rebuild from the past and what to reimagine for the present and future. There were new insights gained from the traumatic experience of being in exile. The people's understanding of who God was and their purpose in the world was maturing and developing. They came home, first to rebuild the temple, then to rebuild the walls and, in the process, to rebuild their identity as God's people.

The Bible shows us a complicated picture of people coming to ever-greater understanding of who God is as they journey on with him, through settled and unsettled times. Through the prophets writing after the exile, they catch renewed glimpses of their purpose to bless all people on earth, the purpose that had been there from the very early days of Abram.

How ready are you to keep learning new things about God?

#jesusjourney
   What temples are best not rebuilt?

14

Radio silence

'I, the Lord, promise to send the prophet Elijah before that great and terrible day comes. He will lead children and parents to love each other more, so that when I come, I won't bring doom to the land.'
MALACHI 4

Jesus Christ came from the family of King David and also from the family of Abraham. And this is a list of his ancestors. From Abraham to King David, his ancestors were...
MATTHEW 1

The last book of the Old Testament is Malachi, one of the prophets. The next book in most Bibles is the New Testament book of Matthew. Between the two are about 400 years. Malachi writes about the – once more – dire state of religious life (are you banging your head against a convenient wall yet?) and predicts a great messenger coming to clean up the nation's act and make things ready for God. Malachi builds a bridge into the future as he sees glimpses of either John the Baptist or Jesus himself in this 'prophet Elijah' character. Matthew starts the same bridge from the other end, looking back down Jesus' family tree as far back as Abraham himself, where so many journeys began.

Is this 400 years of silence another sort of desert into which God draws those who follow God? Instead of great silent skies and wide windswept wildernesses, could this part of the journey be the silence to get ready for the greatest step-change of all?

As Malachi despairs of religious faith that has lost its way, Matthew looks back in wonder from the other side of the divide, to see God's faithfulness to his people, as God walks with them through geography and history towards the restored relationship that was intended. God is always there, guiding, providing, warning, inspiring, challenging and loving, until the time is right for God – even God! – to take an even more significant journey.

Look backwards and forwards in your own life. What milestones mark the journey you've been on so far? What milestone are you walking towards at the moment?

#jesusjourney
What keeps you going when God is silent?

New Testament

15

The longest journey

The true light that shines on everyone was coming into the world. The Word was in the world, but no one knew him, though God had made the world with his Word. He came into his own world, but his own nation did not welcome him. Yet some people accepted him and put their faith in him. So he gave them the right to be the children of God... The Word became a human being and lived here with us. We saw his true glory, the glory of the only Son of the Father. From him all the kindness and all the truth of God have come down to us.

JOHN 1

The gospel writers all begin their accounts of Jesus from different perspectives. Matthew goes back down the family tree; Mark begins with the prophet Isaiah and John the Baptist; Luke starts with John the Baptist's parents and John starts with a new 'In the beginning', using symbolic language trying to describe the way God travelled to earth.

What a strange journey, to go from one dimension to another! John grapples with the concept of the maker of the world coming into the created world; with the light from the first day of creation bursting once again into a dark world; with a story becoming a person and entering the storyteller's own story. God left home and joined us on earth for a season so that one day we can join God in the heavenly home prepared for us for an eternity.

When we reflect on our own journey of life, even the most adventurous of us can't claim to have made a journey on this scale. If journeying with Jesus brings hardships, nothing can compare with the hardships Jesus chose to endure for the sake of love, when he 'lived here with us'.

Think about this on your bus, car or train journeys today, or as you move in a different way from one place to another.

#jesusjourney
   How would Airbnb describe earth?

16

A time of journeys

About that time Emperor Augustus gave orders for the names of all the people to be listed in record books… Everyone had to go to their own hometown to be listed. So Joseph had to leave Nazareth in Galilee and go to Bethlehem in Judea. Long ago Bethlehem had been King David's hometown, and Joseph went there because he was from David's family. Mary was engaged to Joseph and traveled with him to Bethlehem. She was soon going to have a baby, and while they were there, she gave birth to her first-born son. She dressed him in baby clothes and laid him on a bed of hay, because there was no room for them in the inn.

LUKE 2

A new beginning often brings upheavals, like the gun going off at the start of a race. Jesus' birth triggers several journeys. Mary sets off after the angel's visit to see her cousin Elizabeth. Joseph and Mary travel to Bethlehem. The shepherds travel in from the hills outside the town. The wise men journey from the east. And before they can go home to Nazareth, Mary, Joseph and Jesus escape the slaughter of the young boys instigated by Herod and become refugees in Egypt. The pattern has begun again in one family group, as Jesus and his parents travel from their homeland to Egypt and back home. Jesus walked the journey of his ancestors before he was old enough to spell 'pyramid'. For every journey, material possessions would have been left behind, goodbyes would have needed to be said, ties would need to be broken and it would have cost money.

It's as if would-be followers of Jesus are being warned that following him means being on the move in some way. A settled home is something to aspire to, but for those who say 'yes' to God, the safety of home may be something they are asked to give up to further God's purposes. Following Jesus might involve staying put in one place but being constantly on the move in our spirit, open to learning new things, open to changing our attitude, willing to leave behind what holds us back.

How does that grab you?

#jesusjourney
    Are you a brake or an accelerator?

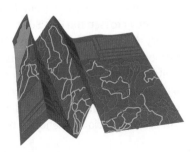

17
Baptism

John the Baptist showed up in the desert and told everyone, 'Turn back to God and be baptised! Then your sins will be forgiven.' From all Judea and Jerusalem crowds of people went to John. They told how sorry they were for their sins, and he baptised them in the Jordan River... About that time Jesus came from Nazareth in Galilee, and John baptised him in the Jordan River. As soon as Jesus came out of the water, he saw the sky open and the Holy Spirit coming down to him like a dove. A voice from heaven said, 'You are my own dear Son, and I am pleased with you.'

MARK 1

At significant moments in their history, the people of God had to go through water to move from the established way of life to the new. They crossed the Red Sea to mark the difference between slavery and freedom. They crossed the River Jordan to mark the difference between being nomads in the wilderness and being a settled people in a land of their own. Here, we see Jesus with his cousin John at the River Jordan, insisting on baptism to mark the difference between his old job as a carpenter and his new role as Messiah. It's another new beginning as the waters of creation sweep over his head and he comes to the surface, as if passing from death to life.

While the rest of humanity might choose to be baptised to mark the forgiveness of sins, Jesus has no sin to forgive. For him, baptism is a sign that he identifies completely as a human being. God independently identifies him as God's own Son in the voice from heaven. Fully human and fully God, Jesus can begin his unique work.

Each time you turn on a tap today, think about the journey that water has made to get to you and the other journeys going on around you in the natural world.

#jesusjourney
Special offer: one part of your past life washed away! What will it be?

18

Journey into the desert

The Holy Spirit led Jesus into the desert, so that the devil could test him. After Jesus had gone without eating for forty days and nights, he was very hungry. Then the devil came to him and said, 'If you are God's Son, tell these stones to turn into bread.' Jesus answered, 'The Scriptures say: "No one can live only on food. People need every word that God has spoken"'... Then the devil left Jesus, and angels came to help him.

MATTHEW 4

Jesus is completely human. The gospel-writers also identify him not just as one person but as a one-man symbol for the whole of God's chosen people. Where the people of God took the wrong turn in the past, the Son of God will take the right turn every time, even when the temptation to take the easy way is strongest. Jesus, like the people of God, is guided out by the Holy Spirit, into the desert, where he spends not 40 years but 40 days. He is given the choice between faithfulness to the job he is called to and, in turn, skewing his powers to make himself comfortable, being a celebrity and being rich and powerful beyond anybody's dreams.

Jesus faces all these temptations head-on but knows, even in his physically weakest moments, who he is and what he is there to do. With 30 years of prayer, examples of faithful living from his family and village and diligent study of scriptures under his belt, he can stay true to who he is meant to be.

Could you allow yourself to be guided into a wilderness space to understand who you really are?

#jesusjourney
   Is it time to plan a retreat or quiet day?

19
Follow me

As Jesus was walking along the shore of Lake Galilee, he saw Simon and his brother Andrew. They were fishermen and were casting their nets into the lake. Jesus said to them, 'Come with me! I will teach you how to bring in people instead of fish.' Right then the two brothers dropped their nets and went with him.

Jesus walked on and soon saw James and John, the sons of Zebedee. They were in a boat, mending their nets. At once Jesus asked them to come with him. They left their father in the boat with the hired workers and went with him.

MARK 1

A teenage friend posted photo after photo of herself at Butlin's with a member of a pop group she'd been following on Twitter and had finally got to meet in the flesh. She couldn't stop talking about him. If he'd said, 'Leave school and come with me,' no question, she'd have done it!

How do you react if someone says, 'Come with me'? I guess it all depends on who it is and how they say it. If it's someone you already think is the bee's knees, someone you've been talking about incessantly, admiring and wishing you could spend more time with, someone it's an unbelievable honour to be with, you might well drop everything and do just what they said.

For these fishermen and for the other people Jesus invites to follow him, his invitation is an unmissable opportunity. This is their chance to be close to someone they admire and respect, someone like no one they've ever met before. It's a chance to go in a completely new direction. They'd be mad to turn it down. But what is it about Jesus that makes them so sure they're doing the right thing?

Imagine Jesus saying to you, 'Come with me!' How do you react?

#jesusjourney
    How well do you need to know Jesus to follow him?

20

Journey away from home

Jesus went back to Nazareth, where he had been brought up, and as usual he went to the meeting place on the Sabbath. When he stood up to read from the Scriptures, he was given the book of Isaiah the prophet. He opened it and read,

'The Lord's Spirit has come to me, because he has chosen me to tell the good news to the poor. The Lord has sent me to announce freedom for prisoners, to give sight to the blind, to free everyone who suffers, and to say, "This is the year the Lord has chosen."'

Jesus closed the book, then handed it back to the man in charge and sat down. Everyone in the meeting place looked straight at Jesus. Then Jesus said to them, 'What you have just heard me read has come true today.'

LUKE 4

Jesus knows his scriptures inside out and has done since childhood. But he reads them not as dry dusty texts but as living words that show him who he is and what he needs to do. The journey of Jesus arguably began many hundreds of years before, when the psalmists and prophets saw glimpses of what God's greatest Rescuer would need to suffer. It can't have been easy reading for the young Jesus, reading their words and knowing what that would mean for him. But their words also give him confidence, purpose and a single-minded vision that refuses to compromise.

Jesus tells his own village who he is and what he needs to do, but they are so furious with his confidence that they almost kill him. Somehow he gets away. Those who should have known him, trusted him and been chuffed to bits that their own boy was on the road to glory were the very ones who drove him out.

How do you react to Jesus' utter conviction of who he is?

#jesusjourney
   The Bible: alive and kicking or dry and dusty?

21

Teaching on the way

'God blesses those people who depend only on him. They belong to the kingdom of heaven! God blesses those people who grieve. They will find comfort! God blesses those people who are humble. The earth will belong to them! God blesses those people who want to obey him more than to eat or drink. They will be given what they want! God blesses those people who are merciful. They will be treated with mercy! God blesses those people whose hearts are pure. They will see him! God blesses those people who make peace. They will be called his children! God blesses those people who are treated badly for doing right. They belong to the kingdom of heaven.'

MATTHEW 5

Out in the countryside, up on a hilltop, with no religious buildings in sight, Jesus starts teaching people about the new way of thinking he's come to start. Anybody can come and listen; there are no 'in' or 'out' people. This is for everyone, from the very young to the very old, for women as well as men, for those at the bottom of the heap as well as those at the top. While his teaching is based on the character of God from the journey so far, Jesus paints a picture of a new way of understanding God's purposes in the world, a new set of priorities, a new way of coming home to God. Being rich and powerful is no longer the goal: it's the poor and powerless, Jesus says, who will be the winners. It's not those who have it all already, but those who come to God with empty hands who will find satisfaction. It's not the warlords but the peacemakers who will find themselves in God's household.

In Jesus' teachings, the map of what pleases God is turned upside down. His listeners at both the top and the bottom of the social pile are going to need to turn away from old habits and make new starts (technical term: 'repent') if they want to be part of this new journey.

How comfortable do you feel about 'new ways'? Practise being open to new ideas by doing something today that you've never done before.

#jesusjourney
Are you more comfortable with the old or the new?

22

Healing on the way

While Jesus was on his way, people were crowding all around him. In the crowd was a woman who had been bleeding for twelve years. She had spent everything she had on doctors, but none of them could make her well. As soon as she came up behind Jesus and barely touched his clothes, her bleeding stopped. 'Who touched me?' Jesus asked. While everyone was denying it, Peter said, 'Master, people are crowding all around and pushing you from every side.'

But Jesus answered, 'Someone touched me, because I felt power going out from me.' The woman knew that she could not hide, so she came trembling and knelt down in front of Jesus. She told everyone why she had touched him and that she had been healed right away. Jesus said to the woman, 'You are now well because of your faith. May God give you peace!'

LUKE 8

Jesus was so full of the Holy Spirit that the kingdom of God simply happened around him. It just took somebody's faith to reach out to touch him and he could heal and transform by his presence alone. Here he is, called urgently to the deathbed of a young girl, but interrupting his journey to find out who reached out in faith to touch his cloak.

Despite the pressure from everyone around him to move on and do the important job in hand, he knows how important it is to resolve this unexpected situation first. He has healed the woman physically already, but now reassures her of wholeness of life and fullness of restored relationship by making sure she knows he knows her. He is Lord of time itself, knowing just when he can stop and when he needs to move on.

Ask Jesus to let you be a kingdom-bringer wherever you go today.

#jesusjourney
    Who do you know who oozes blessing?

23

Back to the wilderness

That evening the disciples came to Jesus and said, 'This place is like a desert, and it is already late. Let the crowds leave, so they can go to the villages and buy some food.'

Jesus replied, 'They don't have to leave. Why don't you give them something to eat?'

But they said, 'We have only five small loaves of bread and two fish.' Jesus asked his disciples to bring the food to him, and he told the crowd to sit down on the grass. Jesus took the five loaves and the two fish. He looked up towards heaven and blessed the food. Then he broke the bread and handed it to his disciples, and they gave it to the people.

MATTHEW 14

Long ago, God's faithfulness to people was shown by God providing bread and meat for them in the desert (look back at pages 18–19). Here, Jesus shows who he is and that he stands in the tradition of Moses, by doing something very similar. The disciples are all for packing the people off, hungry as they are, so they can fend for themselves. Jesus wants them to understand something both about their own responsibilities as his followers and about his compassionate power that longs for people to stay close to him where their needs can be met: 'They do not need to go away. You give them something to eat.'

The people of God are on a journey again, a journey of relearning how much God cares for them and wants to provide for them, blessing them through everyday gifts of staple food. If people were fed years ago by God's own hand and Jesus is here feeding people by his own hand, what does that hint about who Jesus is?

Pause before your next meal and thank God for what it represents.

#jesusjourney
   Most joyful meal?

24
A different sort of wilderness walk

When [the disciples] saw [Jesus walking on the lake], they thought he was a ghost. They were terrified and started screaming. At once, Jesus said to them, 'Don't worry! I am Jesus. Don't be afraid.'

Peter replied, 'Lord, if it is really you, tell me to come to you on the water.'

'Come on!' Jesus said. Peter then got out of the boat and started walking on the water towards him. But when Peter saw how strong the wind was, he was afraid and started sinking. 'Save me, Lord!' he shouted.

Right away, Jesus reached out his hand. He helped Peter up and said, 'You surely don't have much faith. Why do you doubt?'

MATTHEW 14

The sea, for the disciples – seasoned fishermen though some of them were – is a place of danger, where the deeps represented the untamed, godless powers of evil. It is a wilderness like the desert, to be crossed with care, where you take your life in your hands. God had provided a dry path through the dangerous sea in the nation's past, but the sea is something to treat with deep caution.

In this story, the disciples are awed by Jesus demonstrating his power over even the sea. He makes his own rules. He can walk all over any malevolent powers because he is fully Creator God as well as fully created human being. Just as he proves when he calms the storm, the natural world is subject to him – not the other way around. What journey does he encourage Peter on here? This is a step into the unknown in a dramatically different dimension. Peter almost manages it but not quite: the old fears prove too much for his new faith and Jesus needs to rescue him.

What old fears might stop you 'walking on water' somehow today?*

#jesusjourney
   Walking on water: showing off or showing… what?

*BRF is not responsible for any effects of injudicious
   attempts to actually walk on actual water.

25

Changed lives on the way

So [Zacchaeus] ran ahead and climbed up into a sycamore tree. When Jesus got there, he looked up and said, 'Zacchaeus, hurry down! I want to stay with you today.' Zacchaeus hurried down and gladly welcomed Jesus... 'I will give half of my property to the poor. And I will now pay back four times as much to everyone I have ever cheated.'

Jesus said to Zacchaeus, 'Today you and your family have been saved, because you are a true son of Abraham. The Son of Man came to look for and to save people who are lost.'

LUKE 19

Nobody approves of Jesus' going to the house of this distinctly dodgy geezer. Surely, they mutter, Jesus should be more discriminating about the company he keeps. But Jesus knows what he's come for. He wants to set people free from what holds them back from living the best life possible. He wants communities to be transformed. That's what God's rescue (technical term: 'salvation') is all about. He knows he has the power to set Zacchaeus free, simply by going and letting the kingdom happen in Zacchaeus' household.

At the end of the meal, not only is Zacchaeus a changed man but his actions transform the community of Jericho as well, as justice is done and people are repaid the money that has been stolen from them. Jesus knows exactly who he is and what he's been put on earth to do, and isn't swayed by anyone else's opinion.

In the Old Testament, Jericho is conquered by God's power and by force. In the New, it is invaded by love and justice.

How can you bring a taste of that 'salvation invasion' to someone you meet today?

#jesusjourney
    What do you think Zacchaeus did the day after?

26

Off you go!

Jesus called together his twelve apostles and gave them complete power over all demons and diseases. Then he sent them to tell about God's kingdom and to heal the sick. He told them, 'Don't take anything with you! Don't take a walking stick or a traveling bag or food or money or even a change of clothes. When you are welcomed into a home, stay there until you leave that town. If people won't welcome you, leave the town and shake the dust from your feet as a warning to them.' The apostles left and went from village to village, telling the good news and healing people everywhere.

LUKE 9

Following Jesus involved plenty of time in his company, watching him at work, listening to his teaching and stories, observing how he treated people and absorbing his priorities and attitudes. The disciples saw first-hand the power he had and learned how he used it. But Jesus gave them the chance to use that power themselves. He equipped them and sent them out to do the work he was doing. I wonder why? Perhaps Jesus was overwhelmed by the neediness of the people he met and frustrated that he was only one person and could only do so much in one day. At least sending out the disciples would mean a twelve-times bigger impact. Perhaps he had in mind what the disciples were going to need after he had left them: confidence, authority and hands-on experience. Jesus knew exactly how fallible and unprepared his followers were, but he trusted them with the work of the kingdom anyway.

Followers of Jesus can expect to be sent out to do work that seems ridiculously beyond their capabilities. Does that terrify you or excite you?

#jesusjourney

Jesus never said to any of his apprentices, 'You're fired!', because…

27
Hospitality on the way

The Lord and his disciples were traveling along and came to a village. When they got there, a woman named Martha welcomed him into her home. She had a sister named Mary, who sat down in front of the Lord and was listening to what he said. Martha was worried about all that had to be done. Finally, she went to Jesus and said, 'Lord, doesn't it bother you that my sister has left me to do all the work by myself? Tell her to come and help me!'

The Lord answered, 'Martha, Martha! You are worried and upset about so many things, but only one thing is necessary. Mary has chosen what is best, and it will not be taken away from her.'

LUKE 10

Jesus and his disciples are on the road, doing the equivalent of sofa-surfing, reliant on the hospitality of friends and strangers. It is potentially a very vulnerable position to be in as you enter a household with somebody else's rules and priorities. It must have been tempting to compromise on your principles for the sake of politeness to your host. Almost certainly, the disciples would have been uncomfortable that Mary was sitting listening to Jesus, putting herself – a woman – on a level with the disciples themselves – the men. Absolutely certainly, Martha was uncomfortable with it. Her household, her rules.

But Jesus was rewriting the rule book, not on scrolls but in people's hearts. He never left his principles behind as he *was* those principles in his very nature. If there was oppression, he challenged it and offered a new way of living. Women, he made clear, should be encouraged to learn too, to be close to Jesus, to be equal with men.

When we invite Jesus into our household lives, what rules might he want to challenge?

#jesusjourney
  Are you with Martha or Mary?

28
Staying put

A man by the name of Lazarus was sick in the village of Bethany. He had two sisters, Mary and Martha. The sisters sent a message to the Lord and told him that his good friend Lazarus was sick…

When Jesus heard this, he said, 'His sickness won't end in death. It will bring glory to God and his Son.' Jesus loved Martha and her sister and brother. But he stayed where he was for two more days. Then he said to his disciples, 'Now we will go back to Judea.'
JOHN 11

Jesus travels. So it's particularly odd when he could be on the move – when people think he should be on the move – but he stays put. His friends, Mary and Martha, send a message to Jesus that their brother Lazarus is ill. Surely Jesus will set out to heal him? He's done that for people he didn't even know personally! But Jesus stays where he is for two more days. His disciples try to discourage him from going back as he faced danger there; both Martha and Mary tell him that if he had been there, Lazarus would not have died; everybody knows better than Jesus what he should do. But Jesus is so confident of what his Father wants to reveal through the death of Lazarus that he stops, for as long as he knows he needs to, and travels on when he knows he needs to. As a result, Lazarus is not simply healed but brought back to life, and God's glory is revealed in a new way.

Ask God to come so close to you that you too will have Jesus' confidence about when to stay put and when to move on.

#jesusjourney
God's timing: wishful thinking?

29

Stories from the road

Jesus replied: 'As a man was going down from Jerusalem to Jericho, robbers attacked him… A priest happened to be going down the same road. But when he saw the man, he walked by on the other side. Later a temple helper came to the same place. But when he saw the man who had been beaten up, he also went by on the other side.

'A man from Samaria then came traveling along that road. When he saw the man, he felt sorry for him and went over to him. He treated his wounds with olive oil and wine and bandaged them. Then he put him on his own donkey and took him to an inn, where he took care of him.'

LUKE 10

Jesus used the world around him as the settings for his parables. It would be quite fun to imagine that he had travelled this road himself and even perhaps encountered real-life robbers on it. Maybe some of those ex-offenders formed part of the crowd following him and listening to the story… But I digress.

How do we behave towards others when we are following Jesus' way? Like the priest or like the outsider, the Samaritan? Perhaps, too, this story asks how we understand God's compassion for a human race beaten up and battered by its journey? 'Love the Lord your God… and love your neighbour yourself' is the summary of the 'map' of the Old Testament (see Matthew 22). Jesus could fulfil both these commandments perfectly because he was both God and a human being. In this story, he shows us what that love looks like in practice. The risky, costly, boundary-breaking love shown by the mythical Samaritan, if replicated in every follower of Jesus, could heal and restore more than just one lonely traveller.

Take a step across the road to someone in need today.

#jesusjourney
    Who's your neighbour?

30

Stories for the road home

'Not long after that, the younger son packed up everything he owned and left for a foreign country, where he wasted all his money in wild living. He had spent everything, when a bad famine spread through that whole land. Soon he had nothing to eat... Finally, he came to his senses and said, "... I will go to my father."

'The younger son got up and started back to his father. But when he was still a long way off, his father saw him and felt sorry for him. He ran to his son and hugged and kissed him.'

LUKE 15

This parable is set next to the parable of the shepherd going on a journey to find the lost sheep. In both parables, one character gets lost. The sheep is just a fallible, slightly dense sheep and obviously needs looking after by the shepherd. But the younger son in this story is a human being and responsible for much more than just physically getting lost: he makes destructive choices that break down family relationships and destroy resources. Surely this man should be punished – in the old story, the punishment for Israel was exile, being thrown out of home. So surely Jesus' parable will end in the son being exiled from the family home?

But in Jesus' new kingdom, the father, the ultimate authority, goes on a costly journey himself to welcome his son back home. It's the older brother who finds it harder to accept that restoration and forgiveness should happen. Jesus is unequivocal: the Father will give anything for the family to be safe at home together. But how the family members react is left as a challenge and a choice.

Which character in the parable do you most relate to?

#jesusjourney
So… does the older brother join the party?

31

So near!

When Jesus and his disciples were near the town of Caesarea Philippi, he asked them, 'What do people say about the Son of Man?' The disciples answered, 'Some people say you are John the Baptist or maybe Elijah or Jeremiah or some other prophet.'

Then Jesus asked them, 'But who do you say I am?' Simon Peter spoke up, 'You are the Messiah, the Son of the living God.'

Jesus told him: 'Simon, son of Jonah, you are blessed! You didn't discover this on your own. It was shown to you by my Father in heaven. So I will call you Peter, which means "a rock." On this rock I will build my church.'
MATTHEW 16

Bingo! The disciples get it right! Bang on! Their journey with Jesus has taken them through experiences that lead them to absolute certainty, absolute faith, absolute conviction that Jesus is 'the Messiah, the Son of the living God'. This is a mountaintop experience; a high point, a party moment, something to celebrate. The disciples aren't pulled off course by the half-baked ideas of what other people believe: Peter speaks up and simply voices his absolute, rock-solid trust that Jesus is the Messiah. And now that Peter has arrived at that realisation, Jesus can start to map out the future, starting not from stone like the temple, but on one fisherman's God-given faith.

Jesus' question to his disciples is still one with power to shape the journey of the kingdom today. 'Who do you say I am?' he asks, and our answer could be the next stepping stone he needs to advance the kingdom of heaven through us.

As you walk down a road today, picture Jesus walking with you and asking, 'Who do you say I am?'

#jesusjourney
  Rock-solid or quicksand?

32

And yet so far!

From then on, Jesus began telling his disciples what would happen to him. He said, 'I must go to Jerusalem. There the nation's leaders, the chief priests, and the teachers of the Law of Moses will make me suffer terribly. I will be killed, but three days later I will rise to life.'

Peter took Jesus aside and told him to stop talking like that. He said, 'God would never let this happen to you, Lord!'

Jesus turned to Peter and said, 'Satan, get away from me! You're in my way because you think like everyone else and not like God.'

MATTHEW 16

From his giant step forward, his moment of closeness to Jesus, of clear understanding and of arrival at a new stage on the journey, looking to the future, poor Peter takes two steps back. Jesus explains to his disciples just what he's going to have to do to reach his destination. But it's a journey Peter can't accept for this leader he loves. He tries to deflect Jesus from such a disastrous course, but in doing so, becomes the mouthpiece of temptation and is shouted down by Jesus in no uncertain terms. From being so close to Jesus, Peter now seems so out of step with him.

In our journey with Jesus, we can expect to experience something of what Peter did: getting things incredibly right and then incredibly wrong. Peter lets Jesus down but is still forgiven over and over again. He must have been the least arrogant of any church leader since, with that first-hand experience of getting it wrong and being given a second chance. What an example for us as we follow Jesus: we will get it wrong, but we will always be given a second… third… fourth chance to get it right – and the chance to allow others to get it wrong, too.

Being on a journey means getting it wrong from time to time, but is that better than not being on a journey at all?

#jesusjourney
   Why does Jesus build his church on a follower like Peter?

33

Not a picnic in the park

Jesus then told the crowd and the disciples to come closer, and he said: 'If any of you want to be my followers, you must forget about yourself. You must take up your cross and follow me. If you want to save your life, you will destroy it. But if you give up your life for me and for the good news, you will save it. What will you gain, if you own the whole world but destroy yourself? What could you give to get back your soul?'

MARK 8

I mean, why wouldn't everyone drop what they're doing and follow Jesus? Free food in the fresh air, healing at the drop of a hat, witty stories round the campfire, a chance to laugh at those religious leaders who've always looked down their noses at you, a romp against the Romans to look forward to, miracles at every turn: you'd be a fool to stay at home when all that's on offer. Surely?

Almost every person listening to Jesus would have seen a public killing, would have watched condemned prisoners carrying their own crosses to the place of execution. 'Take up your cross!' might even have been an order they'd actually heard barked by Roman soldiers. Here, Jesus sets his face towards Jerusalem and the brutal reality of the journey ahead of him. He doesn't pretend to his followers that their way will be any easier. Instead, he makes sure anyone thinking about signing up as a disciple knows it will be a far-from-easy ride. Is it a journey worth carrying on with if everything you have, everything you are, your life itself, has to be surrendered up and irrevocably destroyed?

Jesus only had the right to ask everything of his disciples because he went there first. As he stands with his disciples and the undecided crowd at the crossroads, he points down the road he's taking himself and makes sure they all know what is involved if they choose to follow him down it.

As you think about your journey with Jesus, is it worth it?

#jesusjourney
  'Take up your cross': what shape is your cross?

34

Journey to Jerusalem

The disciples left and did what Jesus had told them to do. They brought the donkey and its colt and laid some clothes on their backs. Then Jesus got on. Many people spread clothes in the road, while others put down branches which they had cut from trees. Some people walked ahead of Jesus and others followed behind. They were all shouting,

'Hooray for the Son of David! God bless him who comes in the name of the Lord. Hooray for God in heaven above!'

When Jesus came to Jerusalem, everyone in the city was excited and asked, 'Who can this be?'

MATTHEW 21

A new journey to mark the beginning of the end. Jesus invades Roman-occupied Jerusalem, the city that is, among many other things, the symbolic home of God's people. It's an invasion that speaks volumes about the sort of invader Jesus sees himself to be: obedient to God's plan laid down years before in the prophets, non-violent, bringing peace to the city of peace, entering with inexorable gentleness and vulnerability. God is coming home. Just as the whole of the city was amazed when the wise men announced the birth of a king 30 years ago, here too the whole city is affected by his kingly – but odd – arrival. The powerhouses are shaken as the donkey hee-haws and the Romans are not the most nervous.

How does Jesus journey into our lives today? How does he make his home with us? In your experience, does he charge in on a warhorse with a slash-and-burn policy, or does he walk beside you as you go along?

#jesusjourney
  What fat cats does Jesus challenge today?

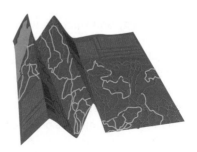

35

Food for the journey ahead

During the meal Jesus took some bread in his hands. He blessed the bread and broke it. Then he gave it to his disciples and said, 'Take this. It is my body.'

Jesus picked up a cup of wine and gave thanks to God. He gave it to his disciples, and they all drank some. Then he said, 'This is my blood, which is poured out for many people, and with it God makes his agreement. From now on I will not drink any wine, until I drink new wine in God's kingdom.'

MARK 14

In the past, God's people were fed on their journey. Jesus reimagines that provision on the hillside for 5,000+ people and offers himself as the bread of life. Now, just before his journey to the cross, he provides food for the journey yet again in the bread and the wine. This symbolic food and drink from the ancient ritual meal of Passover is reimagined by Jesus for his followers. It becomes the provision that will keep them going in the wilderness after he has left them. One physical form leaves them but another is left with them.

What keeps you going on your journey with Jesus? Nobody expects us to keep going on our own. God provides what we need for the journey, although we do have to choose to use it. If we feel as if we're running out of steam, we may find that the gift of Holy Communion, regular Bible reading, prayer or fellowship refreshes us for the next leg.

Which of these provisions might you need to pick up again?

#jesusjourney
   Communion: how is it food for your journey?

36
Journey to the cross

As Jesus was being led away, some soldiers grabbed hold of a man from Cyrene named Simon. He was coming in from the fields, but they put the cross on him and made him carry it behind Jesus. A large crowd was following Jesus, and in the crowd a lot of women were crying and weeping for him...

Jesus shouted, 'Father, I put myself in your hands!' Then he died. When the Roman officer saw what had happened, he praised God and said, 'Jesus must really have been a good man!' A crowd had gathered to see the terrible sight. Then after they had seen it, they felt brokenhearted and went home. All of Jesus' close friends and the women who had come with him from Galilee stood at a distance and watched.

LUKE 23

Jesus' journey led inexorably to the cross. It wasn't a mistake or a miscalculation that took him there by accident, but a carefully planned route that Jesus had understood and intended from very early on, perhaps all his life. But at the time it must have felt to his followers like a terrible failure, a complete train crash.

Perhaps that's why the twelve disciples are silent – maybe not even present – in this account and why the commentary is left to outsiders: to the women who voice the grief the world itself is feeling and to the foreign Roman centurion who sees Jesus' uniqueness even in the middle of a brutal execution.

We see an outsider brought dramatically close to Jesus in the person of Simon of Cyrene. Simon Peter has let Jesus down by saying three times that he didn't know him. A second Simon, a foreigner, not one of the twelve disciples, walks with Jesus, literally carrying his cross, as Jesus had promised his disciples they would need to.

What is the author of Luke saying about following Jesus here?

#jesusjourney
    What's been your experience of dead ends?

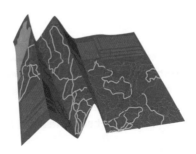

37

Journey from death to life

Very early on Sunday morning the women went to the tomb, carrying the spices that they had prepared. When they found the stone rolled away from the entrance, they went in. But they did not find the body of the Lord Jesus, and they did not know what to think.

Suddenly two men in shining white clothes stood beside them. The women were afraid and bowed to the ground. But the men said, 'Why are you looking in the place of the dead for someone who is alive? Jesus isn't here! He has been raised from death.'

LUKE 24

If Jesus' journey from heaven to earth was a huge one, how even more epic is this journey he makes from death to life? He knocks down the final dividing wall between the earth and the kingdom of heaven. Here he is indeed 'the gate' (John 10) between one world and another, but also 'the way' (John 14) between them. The impassable barrier that shut Adam and Eve out of Eden has been removed, and the way home to be close to God, to working with God, is now possible. The fiery sword guarding the way has been replaced by messengers in clothes that gleam like lightning, who point the women towards a new reality. The tomb door stands open. The final resting place has become the launchpad for a new adventure.

The women didn't understand everything straight away. The male disciples who came later certainly didn't. What made no sense at all to them on that first Easter Sunday gradually came into focus over the next few days and weeks, as they met the risen Jesus and saw for themselves that even death itself couldn't stop God's Son.

What does Jesus' journey here mean to you?

#jesusjourney
    If Jesus came back from the dead…

38

Journey of discovery

That same day two of Jesus' disciples were going to the village of Emmaus, which was about seven miles from Jerusalem. As they were talking and thinking about what had happened, Jesus came near and started walking along beside them. But they did not know who he was...

After Jesus sat down to eat, he took some bread. He blessed it and broke it. Then he gave it to them. At once they knew who he was, but he disappeared... So they got right up and returned to Jerusalem.

LUKE 24

It is still Easter Day and two of Jesus' followers are making their way back home in bafflement. Like Simon Peter returning to his fishing at the end of John's gospel, it's a very human habit, to return to what's familiar after a traumatic event, to try to go home. But for these two disciples, the very journey home turns into a journey of discovery as Jesus himself walks beside them, making sense of all the bewildering happenings of the last few days. As Jesus explains the bigger picture, it all falls into place for them and their frustration turns to excitement. The journey ends with breaking bread together, which reveals Jesus to them.

This experience can't be kept under wraps and it motivates them to set out once more, this time back to Jerusalem, back to the other disciples, to find that they are not the only ones to have met the risen Jesus.

What a journey: from confusion, through the scriptures, to a brand-new recognition of Jesus. Who is walking alongside you to help you understand more about Jesus?

#jesusjourney
The writer/artist/scientist/minister/friend who has opened up the Bible to me is…

39

Get going!

Jesus' eleven disciples went to a mountain in Galilee, where Jesus had told them to meet him. They saw him and worshipped him, but some of them doubted.

Jesus came to them and said: 'I have been given all authority in heaven and on earth! Go to the people of all nations and make them my disciples. Baptise them in the name of the Father, the Son, and the Holy Spirit, and teach them to do everything I have told you. I will be with you always, even until the end of the world.'
MATTHEW 28

The disciples walk to the top of a mountain, aware that mountaintops are the place where significant moments can happen for God's people. While God once gave Moses the commandments on a mountaintop, Jesus now gives his followers a new commandment, a new rule to live by. He sends the disciples off to start a new journey, giving them a new authority and a new purpose. The kingdom of heaven is to grow through these extraordinary ordinary people who have nothing to recommend them but a close relationship with Jesus, a commitment to follow him and his call and authority to go, make disciples, baptise and teach. Their adventure with Jesus is over and their adventure with Jesus is only just beginning. 'Go... I will be with you,' says Jesus to his first followers before he leaves them: what a set of apparently contradictory statements.

What does the adventure mean to you? As you look back at some of these journeys on the Bible so far, which ones resonate with you? Do you have a sense of God calling you to set out into something new or to stay on the road you're already on?

#jesusjourney
My last mountaintop experience was...

40

Rocket launcher

On the day of Pentecost all the Lord's followers were together in one place. Suddenly there was a noise from heaven like the sound of a mighty wind! It filled the house where they were meeting. Then they saw what looked like fiery tongues moving in all directions, and a tongue came and settled on each person there. The Holy Spirit took control of everyone, and they began speaking whatever languages the Spirit let them speak…

[Peter said,] 'Turn back to God! Be baptised in the name of Jesus Christ, so that your sins will be forgiven. Then you will be given the Holy Spirit.'

ACTS 2

Another moment of stillness in the story of God's people. Jesus leaves his disciples – behind on the mountain, goes back to heaven and… nothing happens.

But instead of the half-hearted failure of religion that Malachi bewailed at the end of the Old Testament, the disciples have the covenant relationship in their minds and hearts, just as Jeremiah had predicted. They go off to pray and praise God.

And it is in the middle of one of their gatherings of prayer and praise that this game-changing moment happens. The Holy Spirit of Jesus comes down like a tidal wave. In one morning, the journey from looking inwards to looking outwards has begun again. From a room with closed doors, the disciples spill out into the streets of the city, sharing the good news of Jesus, inviting everyone from every nation to join them on the journey with him.

What sort of a journey would this be? The disciples didn't know. They just had to follow where the Spirit led them, improvising under his guidance, piecing together the clues from their understanding of scripture to make sense of this new journey.

Are you ready for a new direction?

#jesusjourney
How comfortable are you with improvising?

41
Making it up as we go along

They spent their time learning from the apostles, and they were like family to each other. They also broke bread and prayed together.

Everyone was amazed by the many miracles and wonders that the apostles worked. All the Lord's followers often met together, and they shared everything they had. They would sell their property and possessions and give the money to whoever needed it. Day after day they met together in the temple. They broke bread together in different homes and shared their food happily and freely, while praising God. Everyone liked them, and each day the Lord added to their group others who were being saved.

ACTS 2

It's like settling into a new promised land! Instead of a river to cross, the new believers go through baptism. They now have a new lifestyle to work out as they establish themselves as God's people, Jesus' people, people of the Holy Spirit. The new way of life is based on what their new leaders can teach them, people who had actually walked with Jesus. They do everything together to help each other grow in their relationship with God and to pour out God's love to the needy around them. Their very way of life is a sign of the sort of kingdom they stand for; it is a living demonstration of Jesus' heart. The early followers of Jesus get on with doing what Jesus used to do, but now there are several thousand of them to do it, and the number is growing every day.

This was a journey in reverse: instead of the people of God walking to a new country, the new kingdom grew wherever they went.

This same Holy Spirit is at work in the followers of Jesus today. How do you see this kingdom of compassion and justice growing?

#jesusjourney

Clues that the Holy Spirit's at work: …

42

The going gets tough

But Stephen was filled with the Holy Spirit. He looked towards heaven, where he saw our glorious God and Jesus standing at his right side. Then Stephen said, 'I see heaven open and the Son of Man standing at the right side of God!'

The council members shouted and covered their ears. At once they all attacked Stephen and dragged him out of the city. Then they started throwing stones at him. The men who had brought charges against him put their coats at the feet of a young man named Saul.

As Stephen was being stoned to death, he called out, 'Lord Jesus, please welcome me!' He knelt down and shouted, 'Lord, don't blame them for what they have done.' Then he died.

ACTS 7

It was all going so well. The new church could do so much to be the hands and feet of Jesus in the city. But just as the Old Testament people of God were taken on journey after journey, so the new family of God is kept on the move. The new movement provokes fury among the traditionalists like Saul. The old tries to stamp out the new. Its pioneers are brought to trial and even executed, like Stephen here.

The persecution, tragic though it must have felt to those close-knit early believers, had another dynamic effect, which was to send the believers out of the Jerusalem centre back to the different places they came from. As we have seen, the new kingdom wasn't reliant on geographical space: everywhere a believer went, the kingdom went too and spread from her or him to those around them. Jesus' kingdom was on the move.

New Christians often encounter strong opposition in the early days of their decision to follow Jesus. What opposition do you face?

#jesusjourney
   Pray for those persecuted for their faith, especially…

43

An unexpected passenger

Saul kept on threatening to kill the Lord's followers. He even went to the high priest and asked for letters to the Jewish leaders in Damascus. He did this because he wanted to arrest and take to Jerusalem any man or woman who had accepted the Lord's Way. When Saul had almost reached Damascus, a bright light from heaven suddenly flashed around him. He fell to the ground and heard a voice that said, 'Saul! Saul! Why are you so cruel to me?'

'Who are you?' Saul asked.

'I am Jesus,' the Lord answered. 'I am the one you are so cruel to.'

ACTS 9

Imagine your sailing ship is taken over by ruthless pirates. But suddenly the chief pirate throws off his parrot and claims he wants to use his navigational skills to be part of your crew and help you get wherever you were sailing. Something of that nature happened to the early Christians, small in number, largely made up of slaves and riff-raff, scattered across the country, hiding from persecution by the religious authorities. The person most intent on wiping them out claims to have met Jesus himself and now wants to help the people he was viciously attacking. Saul is the least likely person to follow Jesus, but Jesus calls him anyway. What a challenge for the followers of the Way, as they were known before anyone invented the word 'Christian', especially as they would all know somebody injured, imprisoned or killed by Saul's intervention. What a sacrifice Jesus asked them to make in accepting Saul (who was later renamed Paul) as one of them.

Jesus sends all sorts of people to join the church. We don't get to pick and choose the people we fancy. We are asked to welcome everyone unconditionally. After all, they could, like Paul, turn out to be an unexpected blessing.

Who do you need to welcome?

#jesusjourney
My ideal church
would consist of...

44

A bigger map

While Peter was still speaking, the Holy Spirit took control of everyone who was listening. Some Jewish followers of the Lord had come with Peter, and they were surprised that the Holy Spirit had been given to Gentiles. Now they were hearing Gentiles speaking unknown languages and praising God.

Peter said, 'These Gentiles have been given the Holy Spirit, just as we have! I am certain that no one would dare stop us from baptising them.' Peter ordered them to be baptised in the name of Jesus Christ, and they asked him to stay on for a few days.

ACTS 10

The new Jesus-followers have to look at everything through a new set of spectacles. The old 'maps' – the scriptures and religious structures – are a great starting place but aren't big enough anymore. In the book of Acts and the letters that follow, we see the new Christians gradually unrolling the map of the new adventure. They really are the followers of the Way. We see them grappling with the sheer scale of the vision that Jesus' death and resurrection has opened up.

One such huge opening up of horizons is the understanding that a covenant relationship with God belongs not just to people from a Jewish heritage (technical term: 'the circumcised') but, through Jesus' work, to everyone from every other people group (technical term: 'Gentiles' or non-Jewish people) – the Gentiles, as non-Jewish people were known. It took a while for the early church to come to terms with what God was doing. Some people take a lot more convincing to leave the old ways behind. Some, even in the new church, had more to lose by opening the doors to everyone.

What new ideas are you grappling with at the moment? Ask Jesus to help you understand your true motives in the struggle.

#jesusjourney
   Power: take it or leave it?

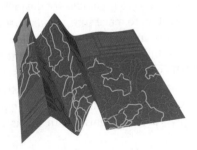

45

Changing the map

On the Sabbath we went outside the city gate to a place by the river, where we thought there would be a Jewish meeting place for prayer. We sat down and talked with the women who came. One of them was Lydia, who was from the city of Thyatira and sold expensive purple cloth. She was a worshiper of the Lord God, and he made her willing to accept what Paul was saying. Then after she and her family were baptised, she kept on begging us, 'If you think I really do have faith in the Lord, come stay in my home.' Finally, we accepted her invitation.

ACTS 16

How did the story spread from one tiny group of believers in Jerusalem across the Mediterranean and beyond? In the book of Acts, we see glimpses of the journeys the first church leaders went on to make sure as many people as possible heard about Jesus and learned how to follow him. Paul, Barnabas, Peter and many others set off where the Spirit led them, brushed off shipwrecks, muggings and imprisonment as adventures almost not worth mentioning and settled temporarily in different places. They came, not as conquering empire-builders with swords, or colonists with bricks and mortar, but as empty-handed messengers with words and the Holy Spirit. This 'kingdom' (Jesus' way of describing the way God wants things to be) was a gentle and persuasive one that changed hearts and minds, as we see here in Lydia and her household.

Not many of us think we can start new churches. It might feel as if it's a bit professionalised in the 21st century. But Paul and co didn't wait for permission. They just went and told anybody who would listen what God was doing through Jesus and took it from there. And, perhaps to their surprise, they found that God had gone before them!

What a challenge for us. Perhaps it isn't up to 'someone else' to tell God's story. Perhaps it's up to us.

#jesusjourney
   This is the one thing I want you to know about Jesus: …

46

Working it out as we go along

I have good things to say about Phoebe, who is a leader in the church at Cenchreae... Give my greetings to Priscilla and Aquila. They have not only served Christ Jesus together with me, but they have even risked their lives for me. I am grateful for them and so are all the Gentile churches. Greet the church that meets in their home.

Greet my dear friend Epaenetus, who was the first person in Asia to have faith in Christ. Greet Mary, who has worked so hard for you. Greet my relatives Andronicus and Junia, who were in jail with me. They are highly respected by the apostles and were followers of Christ before I was... Greet Tryphaena and Tryphosa, who work hard for the Lord. Greet my dear friend Persis. She also works hard for the Lord.

ROMANS 16

What do we see in the Bible after the book of Acts, which tells us how the first Jesus-followers talked their way around the

Mediterranean? The next set of books is made up of letters (technical term: 'epistles'). These letters were by the early church leaders writing by and large to people they loved very dearly and had had to leave behind to keep on sharing the story of Jesus in other places. These letters are evidence of how the Christians in those first few decades after Jesus' ministry worked things out together in good and bad times, at home and in prison, in their own households and in their relationship to the government of the day. They contain advice, encouragement, teaching, warnings and personal greetings and they remain helpful for working out how to live as a follower of Jesus today, even though the world around us has moved on so much.

In the short passage above, for example, what can we see about the importance of women in the early church? Look at the risks Paul and his friends ran to follow Jesus. Look at the love between them, which underpinned the hard teaching elsewhere. This isn't a rulebook but a book about relationships being worked out.

Send your love to a Christian who means a lot to you.

#jesusjourney
Which is easier?
Keeping rules or
growing friendships?

47

Steering a course

Timothy… don't let anyone make fun of you, just because you are young. Set an example for other followers by what you say and do, as well as by your love, faith, and purity.

Until I arrive, be sure to keep on reading the Scriptures in worship, and don't stop preaching and teaching. Use the gift you were given when the prophets spoke and the group of church leaders blessed you by placing their hands on you. Remember these things and think about them, so everyone can see how well you are doing. Be careful about the way you live and about what you teach. Keep on doing this, and you will save not only yourself, but the people who hear you.

1 TIMOTHY 4

In Paul's letters, we see the way the early Christians worked out their new lives focused on Jesus. They changed their behaviour as a community and as individuals. Here is part of a letter from Paul to his young friend Timothy, an apprentice church leader, whom Paul has worked with and who is obviously coming across a few pitfalls in his journey to lead a local church well. Paul encourages Timothy to lead by example, to be disciplined, committed and self-critical, for his own sake and for the sake of those he is serving. Again, we see the promise coming true of a covenant with the living God written down in this young leader's heart. We see the way of life the Christians followed is learned from observing each other, as Timothy observed Paul and as Timothy's church needs to observe Timothy himself. It's a community on the move, with each individual member taking personal responsibility to guard their own relationship with God and with each other.

How much responsibility do you take for your own journey with God and for that of those around you?

#jesusjourney
    My prayer for my church leader today: …

48
Navigating wrong turns

I am told that you can't get along with each other when you worship, and I am sure that some of what I have heard is true… When you meet together, you don't really celebrate the Lord's Supper. You even start eating before everyone gets to the meeting, and some of you go hungry, while others get drunk. Don't you have homes where you can eat and drink? Do you hate God's church? Do you want to embarrass people who don't have anything? What can I say to you? I certainly cannot praise you.

1 CORINTHIANS 11

A perfect society? Hardly! In the letters, we read about the early church getting things wrong, falling out, going the wrong way and having to find their way back to God – not just once, but over and over again. Here, Paul is trying to correct some bad habits that the Christians in Corinth had got into. The way they were behaving when they gathered together was socially divisive, elitist, hurtful and chaotic. It wasn't a gathering that showed who Jesus was. This is an example of the early church being free to find their own way and getting it wrong. They needed Paul to come alongside them and point out a better way.

The church of Jesus is on the journey together, like a large family jam-packed into a car. There are arguments and disagreements, but because the family is joined unbreakably by the love they have for each other and, even more powerfully, by the love Jesus pours out on them, they work things out as they travel along together. We get it wrong; we listen to each other's advice; we say sorry and forgive and set off again.

Church means we journey together.
How do you feel about that?

#jesusjourney
Togetherness trumps everything: Y/N

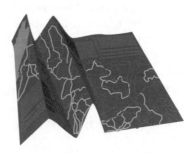

49

The way, the destination

We know what love is because Jesus gave his life for us. That's why we must give our lives for each other. If we have all we need and see one of our own people in need, we must have pity on that person, or else we cannot say we love God. Children, you show love for others by truly helping them, and not merely by talking about it.

1 JOHN 3

Jesus described himself as 'the way' (John 14:6). It's mind-boggling to think of him as both the destination of our journey and the means of getting there. But through the letters of those early 'followers of the way', we see a clue about what that means. Here, John writes about love. It is, he says, a genuine love that reveals itself in how we behave, based on the actions and example of Jesus. The person we want to get closer to – our destination and goal – is Jesus, who is the love of God in human form. And the way we get closer to him is through loving in the same ways as he loved us. Love is the endpoint of our journey and love is the way we get there. No wonder we need to travel in community, as a church, not as lone rangers on our own. How could we learn to love other people if we never had anything to do with them?

The books of the Bible describe the journey of the people of God over thousands of years. There are individual journeys within it, and the overarching theme of an entire people's journey away from God – but led by God through God back to God. Led by love, through love, back to love.

Look out for love today.

#jesusjourney
    Love in action = …

50

Eyes on the horizon

I saw a new heaven and a new earth. The first heaven and the first earth had disappeared, and so had the sea. Then I saw New Jerusalem, that holy city, coming down from God in heaven. It was like a bride dressed in her wedding gown and ready to meet her husband.

I heard a loud voice shout from the throne: 'God's home is now with his people. He will live with them, and they will be his own. Yes, God will make his home among his people. He will wipe all tears from their eyes, and there will be no more death, suffering, crying, or pain. These things of the past are gone forever.'

Then the one sitting on the throne said: 'I am making everything new.'

REVELATION 21

The journey of God's people has been from a perfect home, out across deserts, through water and into a new home. It's taken us on a journey of discovery into what it means to be a people settled into a geographical space but called to keep travelling towards God. We've been exiled from that home and brought back again. Then with Jesus, a new journey begins, one of love in person, living a life of love, walking the path of love, to a goal of love to make it possible for anyone and everyone to experience that love. The new journey of the new people of God begins with the Holy Spirit leading God's people into what it means to love. And here, right at the end of the Bible, we catch a glimpse of what lies beyond the suffering inherent in a life of love: a perfect home where there is nothing but love.

At what point on the journey are you?

#jesusjourney
    Journey of a lifetime or passing phase?

Prayer
    The strength of travelling together
    The compassion that waits
    The companionship of wayside meals
    The freedom of open gates

    The conviction of the only way
    The light shone by the wisest guide
    The stubbornness that keeps you moving
    The compass, map and star to read

    The gentle chat when the pace is slow
    The heady rush when it goes fast
    The open door to welcome you
    The homecooked meal at last
    Be yours.

Church, but not as you know it

BRF's Messy Church is a form of church that
involves creativity, celebration and hospitality,
and enables people of all ages to belong to Christ
together through their local church. It is particularly
aimed at people who have never belonged
to a church before.

Find out more at
messychurch.org.uk

brf.org.uk